NEPTUNE

by Ruth Owen

WINDMILL
BOOKS

New York

Published in 2014 by Windmill Books, An Imprint of Rosen Publishing
29 East 21st Street, New York, NY 10010

Produced for Windmill by Ruby Tuesday Books Ltd
Editor for Ruby Tuesday Books Ltd: Mark J. Sachner
US Editor: Joshua Shadowens
Designer: Trudi Webb and Emma Randall
Consultant: Kevin Yates, Fellow of the Royal Astronomical Society

Photo Credits: Cover, 1, 4–5, 6–7, 11 (bottom), 14–15, 16–17, 18–19, 20–21, 22–23, 25, 26–27 © NASA; 4–5, 6 (bottom), 8–9, 13, 28–29 © Shutterstock; 11 (top) © European Southern Observatory; 12 © Public Domain.

Publisher Cataloging Data

Owen, Ruth.
Neptune / by Ruth Owen.
  p. cm. — (Explore outer space)
Includes index.
ISBN 978-1-61533-729-3 (library binding) — ISBN 978-1-61533-775-0 (pbk.) —
 ISBN 978-1-6153-3776-7 (6-pack)
1. Neptune (Planet) — Juvenile literature. I. Owen, Ruth, 1967–. II. Title.
QB691.O94 2014
523.481—dc23

Manufactured in the United States of America

CPSIA Compliance Information: Batch #BS13WM: For Further Information contact Windmill Books, New York, New York at 1-866-478-0556

CONTENTS

A Very Faraway Planet

Neptune is the most distant **planet** from the Sun in our **solar system**. It **orbits** the Sun at an average distance of 2.8 billion miles (4.5 billion km). That's about 30 times further from the Sun than Earth.

The five planets nearest to Earth, Mercury, Venus, Mars, Jupiter, and Saturn can be seen with the naked eye. Ancient **astronomers** watched and studied these planets for thousands of years. Neptune is too faint from Earth to be seen without a telescope, however. Astronomers did not know this planet existed until the mid 1800s.

Today, we know Neptune is home to massive storms. We know it has many **moons** and is made mostly of gases and liquids. Only one spacecraft has ever visited the planet, though, so we still have much to learn about this huge, icy, distant world.

That's Out of This World!

Neptune's circumference at its **equator** is 96,129 miles (154,705 km) around. If you drove a car at 60 miles per hour (97 km/h) without stopping, a nonstop road trip around Neptune would take nearly 10 weeks. To make the same journey around Earth would take only two weeks.

This image of Neptune was taken by *Voyager 2*, the only spacecraft to have visited the planet.

THE BIRTH OF A PLANET

Neptune and the other planets in the solar system were created when our Sun formed about 4.5 billion years ago.

Before our solar system formed, there was a huge cloud of gas and dust floating in space. Over time, part of the cloud collapsed on itself, forming a massive spinning sphere, or ball. Around the sphere, a disk formed from the remaining gas and dust. The sphere pulled in more gas and dust, adding to its size, weight, and **gravity**. Pressure built up as the material in the sphere was pressed together by gravity, causing the sphere's core to heat up and reach temperatures of around 18 million°F (10 million°C). Finally, the temperature inside the sphere became so hot that it ignited. A new **star**, our Sun, was born!

Gas and dust continued to spin in a disk around the Sun. Over time, this leftover matter from the formation of the Sun clumped together to form the solar system's planets, their moons, **asteroids**, and every other object in our solar system.

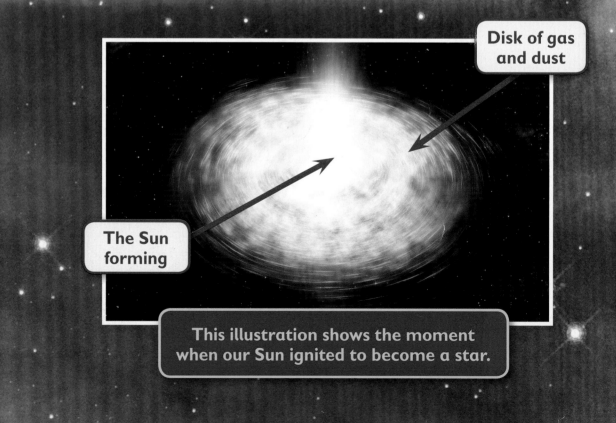

Disk of gas and dust

The Sun forming

This illustration shows the moment when our Sun ignited to become a star.

That's Out of This World!

The clouds of gas and dust where stars begin their lives are called **nebulae**. They form in many different shapes and colors and can be trillions of miles (km) wide. The word nebula is the Latin word for "cloud."

This is part of the Carina Nebula. Nebulae are often called "star factories" or "star nurseries."

Sizing Up the Planets

Mercury is the closest planet to the Sun. Next comes Venus, then Earth, Mars, Jupiter, Saturn, Uranus, and finally Neptune.

It can be difficult to imagine the sizes of the planets. One fun way to compare them is to think of the Sun as a bowling ball. Using that scale, Mercury and Mars would be the size of pinheads compared to the bowling ball Sun. Venus and Earth would be the size of peppercorns. Uranus and Neptune would be the size of peas, while Saturn would be marble-sized. Jupiter, the largest of the planets, would be the size of a chestnut.

The solar system's eight planets do not all have the same structure. Mercury, Venus, Earth, and Mars formed with solid, rocky surfaces. Jupiter, Saturn, Uranus, and Neptune, the furthest planets from the Sun, are made mostly of gas and do not have solid surfaces. These huge planets are known as the gas giants.

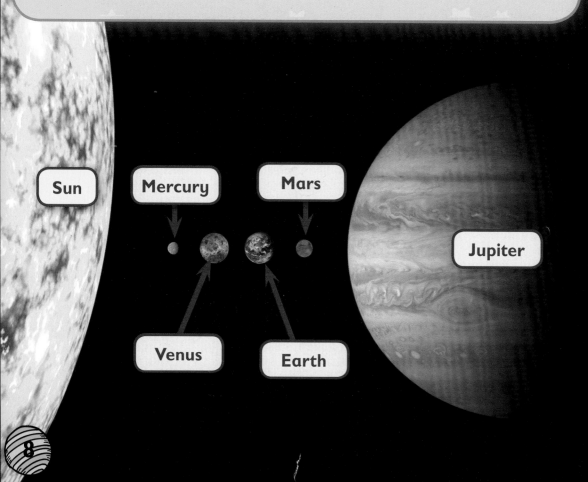

Sun Mercury Mars Jupiter Venus Earth

8

That's Out of This World!

Neptune has a diameter of 30,598 miles (49,243 km).
That's four times the diameter of Earth.

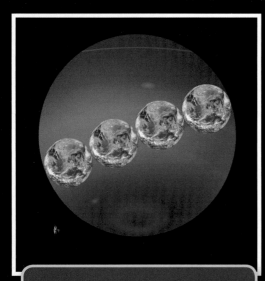

This diagram compares the size of Neptune to Earth.

This diagram shows the sizes of the eight planets to scale. The distances between the planets and the Sun are not to scale.

Saturn

Uranus

Neptune

Imagining the Solar System

Each of the planets in our solar system is orbiting the Sun. The solar system is so vast, however, that it can be hard to imagine the distances between the planets when those distances are measured in millions or billions of miles (km).

So how can we imagine the enormous distances between the Sun and the planets, especially the outer planets such as Neptune? If we once again think of the Sun as a bowling ball, our peppercorn-sized Earth would be about 26 yards (24 m) from the Sun. Faraway pea-sized Neptune, however, would be 777 yards (710 m) from the bowling ball Sun. That's the length of over six football fields!

In 1977, two NASA spacecraft, *Voyager 1* and *Voyager 2*, left Earth. By spring 2011, the *Voyagers* had made it to the outer regions of our solar system. Even though they are traveling at speeds of about 34,000 miles per hour (54,700 km/h), the two spacecraft still took over 30 years just to reach the edge of our solar system.

That's Out of This World!

As Neptune and Earth orbit the Sun, the closest the two planets ever come together during their orbits is about 2.7 billion miles (4.3 billion km).

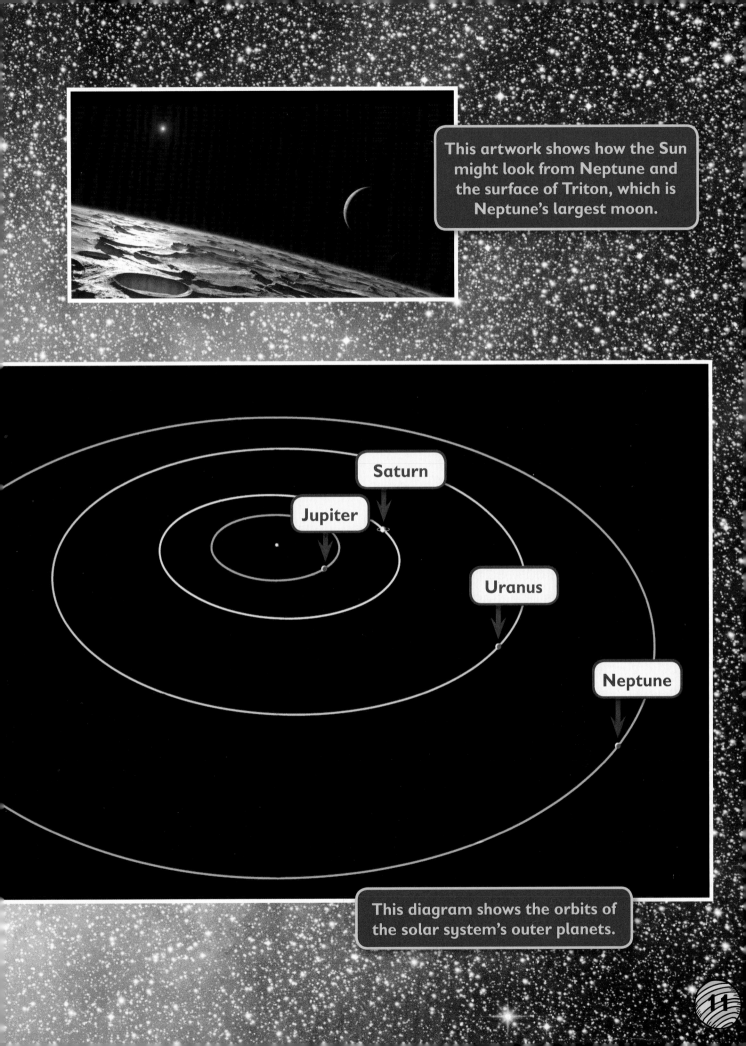

This artwork shows how the Sun might look from Neptune and the surface of Triton, which is Neptune's largest moon.

Saturn

Jupiter

Uranus

Neptune

This diagram shows the orbits of the solar system's outer planets.

The Discovery of Neptune

For centuries, astronomers knew of five planets that could be seen from Earth with the naked eye. Then, in 1781, Uranus became the first planet to be discovered by an astronomer using a telescope.

German-born British astronomer William Herschel discovered Uranus while looking for stars in March 1781. When he first observed the planet, he believed it was a star or perhaps a **comet**.

Just over 50 years later, Neptune was discovered using a combination of math calculations and a telescope. A French mathematician named Urbain Joseph Le Verrier predicted the existence of Neptune when he noticed that the gravity of a large object was affecting the orbit of Uranus. Le Verrier sent his calculations to a German astronomer Johann Gottfried Galle. Using Le Verrier's information, Galle searched for the mysterious object using a telescope and found Neptune on his first night of searching in September 1846.

Urbain Joseph Le Verrier

Johann Gottfried Galle

That's Out of This World!

The Romans named the planets they could see in the sky after their gods Mercury, Venus, Mars, Jupiter, and Saturn. Later, when astronomers discovered "new" planets in the solar system, they continued to name them after ancient gods. Uranus was the Greek god of the sky and Neptune was the Roman god of the sea.

A statue of the Roman god Neptune

NEPTUNE'S DAYS AND YEARS

Like our Earth and every other object in the solar system, distant Neptune is orbiting the Sun. As it travels through space, it is moving at about 12,000 miles per hour (19,300 km/h).

The time period that it takes a planet to make one full orbit of the Sun is called a year. Earth orbits the Sun once every 365 days, so a year on Earth lasts for 365 days. Neptune's journey takes much longer, however, because it is so much farther from the Sun. In order to make one full orbit of the Sun, Neptune must travel 17.5 billion miles (28.2 billion km). This incredible journey takes 60,190 days. So a year on Neptune is nearly 165 Earth years long!

As each planet orbits the Sun, it also spins, or rotates, on its **axis**. Earth rotates once every 24 hours. Neptune rotates faster than Earth, though, and makes one full rotation every 16 hours.

That's Out of This World!

Since Neptune was discovered in 1846, it has only made one full orbit of the Sun. It celebrated its first complete orbit, or year, since its discovery in 2011!

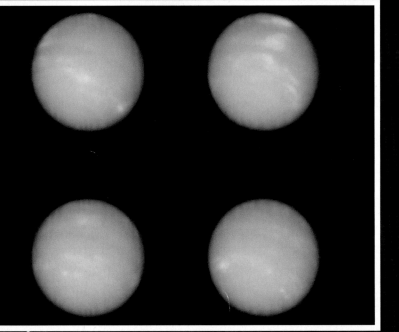

These four images of Neptune were captured by the Hubble Space Telescope on June 25 and 26, 2011. The pictures commemorate the planet's first full orbit since its discovery. One image was taken every four hours as the planet rotated through its 16-hour day.

The Hubble Space Telescope orbits Earth outside of our atmosphere.

Neptune, Inside and Out

As one of the gas giant planets, Neptune does not have a solid surface like Earth or Mars. This planet is made mostly of gases and liquids.

Under a layer of clouds, Neptune has an **atmosphere** of hydrogen, helium, and methane gases. The methane in the planet's atmosphere, and how it behaves with the Sun's light is what gives Neptune its blue color. Light is made up of different colors. When the Sun's light hits Neptune's atmosphere, the methane absorbs the red parts of the light, but reflects the blues and greens, so we see Neptune as blue. Uranus gets its blue color in exactly the same way. Neptune is a much brighter blue than Uranus, however, so scientists still need to discover what causes the difference in the planets' colors.

Beneath Neptune's atmosphere are layers of icy liquid hydrogen, helium, methane, water, and ammonia. At the center of the planet, scientists believe there is a solid core of rock and ice that is about the size of Earth.

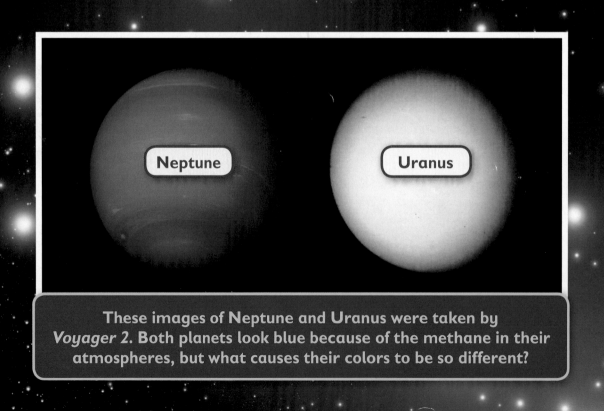

Neptune

Uranus

These images of Neptune and Uranus were taken by *Voyager 2*. Both planets look blue because of the methane in their atmospheres, but what causes their colors to be so different?

That's Out of This World!

Neptune is a huge planet compared to Earth, so you would expect for it to have much greater gravity than Earth. Because it is made of gases and liquid, though, Neptune is very light for its size, so its gravity is only about 10 percent more than Earth's. This means if you weighed 100 pounds (45 kg) on Earth, you would weigh 110 pounds (50 kg) on Neptune.

Inside Neptune

Clouds

Hydrogen, helium, and methane gas

Liquid hydrogen, helium, methane, water, ammonia, and ice

Solid core of rock and metal

A VERY STORMY PLANET

On Earth, the Sun is the driving force behind the many different types of weather that we experience. You would therefore expect that Neptune, which is so much further from the Sun, would simply be icy cold with very little weather. That is not the case, however.

Storms hurtle around Neptune and winds have been recorded at speeds of up to 1,500 miles per hour (2,400 km/h). That's over 10 times the windspeed of the very worst hurricanes here on Earth!

When *Voyager 2* visited Neptune in 1989, it witnessed a huge storm in progress that scientists named the Great Dark Spot. The hurricane-like storm was large enough to contain our Earth. When the Hubble Space Telescope viewed Neptune in 1994, the storm was gone. This was interesting to astronomers because a giant storm named the Great Red Spot has been raging on Jupiter for over 400 years. Neptune's storms seem to form and die down much faster, though, showing how changeable the planet's weather can be.

That's Out of This World!

Neptune's extreme weather could be linked to heat coming from inside the planet. Even though Neptune is much further from the Sun than Uranus and receives about 40 percent less sunlight, both planets have similar surface temperatures. This means Neptune is generating its own internal heat. This heat could be helping to cause the planet's crazy weather!

This image shows three weather features observed by *Voyager 2*: the Great Dark Spot storm, which was moving at about 750 miles per hour (1,200 km/h), fast-moving, bright clouds that were nicknamed Scooter, and a smaller storm called Dark Spot 2.

The Great Dark Spot

Scooter

Dark Spot 2

19

DISTANT MOONS

Just 17 days after Johann Gottfried Galle discovered Neptune in September 1846, the planet's largest moon, Triton, was discovered by a British astronomer named William Lassell.

In 1949, over 100 years later, American astronomer Gerard Kuiper discovered Neptune's third largest moon, Nereid. Nereid has a diameter of just 210 miles (340 km), and is so far from Neptune that it takes 360 days to make one orbit of the planet.

When *Voyager 2* visited Neptune 40 years later, it discovered the planet's second largest moon, Proteus, and five other smaller moons. Even though Proteus, with a diameter of 260 miles (420 km) is larger than Nereid, it was too difficult to see from Earth because it is one of the darkest objects in the solar system. The little moon is covered in **craters** caused by collisions with other space objects.

As technology has improved, astronomers using telescopes on Earth have been able to find more moons orbiting Neptune. At the beginning of 2013, Neptune had a total of 13 known moons.

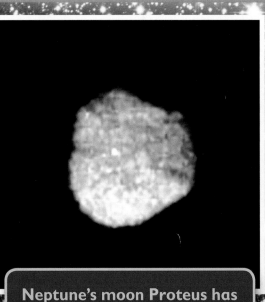

Neptune's moon Proteus has a lumpy, irregular shape.

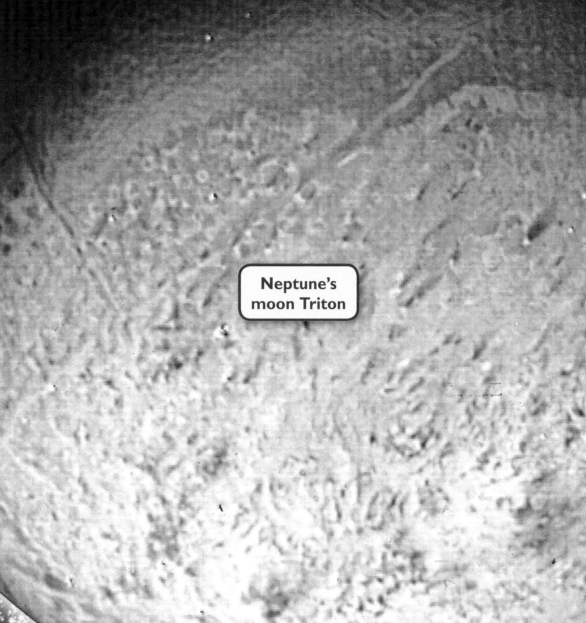

Neptune's moon Triton

That's Out of This World!

Neptune's moons are named after characters from Roman and Greek **myths** that have connections to the ocean or to the gods of the sea, Neptune and Poseidon.

TRITON

Neptune's largest moon, Triton, is about three-quarters the size of Earth's moon. It has a diameter of 1,680 miles (2,700 km).

Triton orbits Neptune in the opposite direction to which the planet is rotating. This is unusual for a large moon and makes scientists think that the moon did not form alongside the planet. It is possible that Triton is an object from a region in space named the **Kuiper Belt**, and was captured by Neptune's gravity and pulled into orbit around the planet.

Triton's crust is made of frozen nitrogen. Beneath the crust is a layer of liquids and ice surrounding a core of rock and metal. Icy liquids, believed to be nitrogen and methane, burst from the moon's crust through **cryovolcanoes**, or ice volcanoes. This material can travel miles (km) into the cold atmosphere surrounding the moon. Then the liquids freeze and snow back down onto the moon's surface.

This scene showing the surface of Triton was created by computers using data from *Voyager 2.*

This image shows the bright, icy surface of Triton.

That's Out of This World!

Triton's surface is so icy it actually reflects most of the sunlight that reaches it instead of absorbing it. This makes the moon one of the coldest places in the solar system. Its surface temperature is about -400°F (-240°C).

NEPTUNE'S RINGS

About a week before William Lassell discovered Triton in 1846, he believed he saw a ring around Neptune. What Lassell in fact saw was a **distortion** of light, or trick, caused by his telescope.

When *Voyager 2* visited Neptune nearly 150 years later, however, it discovered that, like the other gas giants, Jupiter, Saturn, and Uranus, Neptune does indeed have rings. To date, six rings have been discovered encircling Neptune.

Neptune's rings are made of dust and pieces of rock. Unlike Saturn's vast, showy rings, Neptune's rings are thin, dark and very difficult to see. In places, the material in the rings clumps together to form thicker areas called arcs.

Very little is known about Neptune's rings, but scientists believe they may only be a few million years old. They may also not be a permanent feature, but might be forming and then breaking apart, unlike Saturn's more permanent system of rings.

That's Out of This World!

Neptune's gravity is actually pulling its largest moon, Triton, closer and closer to it. It will take millions of years, but eventually Triton may be pulled so close that the force of Neptune's gravity will shatter the moon and Triton may become a ring of rocks and dust encircling the planet!

Neptune's rings

The arcs, or thicker areas, of Neptune's rings can be seen in this image captured by *Voyager* 2.

Arcs

Saturn's rings

Saturn's thick, multiple rings can easily be observed from Earth with a telescope, while Neptune's thin, faint rings are highly difficult to see. The colors in this image have been added by computer.

MISSION TO NEPTUNE

Only one spacecraft, *Voyager 2*, has ever visited Neptune. *Voyager 2* and its sister ship, *Voyager 1*, began their mission to visit the solar system's gas giants in 1977.

The mission was possible because the orbits of Jupiter, Saturn, Uranus, and Neptune were **aligned** in a way that only happens every 175 years. This rare alignment allowed the spacecraft to visit a planet and then use the gravity of that planet like a slingshot to propel them on to their next destination.

Voyager 2 launched from the Kennedy Space Center at Cape Canaveral, Florida, on August 20, 1977. *Voyager 1* actually launched after *Voyager 2* on September 5, 1977.

Originally, the plan was that the two spacecraft would visit Jupiter and Saturn. The *Voyagers* functioned so successfully, however, that it became possible to extend their missions. *Voyager 2* visited Jupiter, then Saturn, and when it was found that its instruments were still functioning well, its mission was extended to include Uranus. After a five and a half hour flyby of Uranus, *Voyager 2* was set on a course for Neptune.

That's Out of This World!

Voyager 2 got its name because even though it launched before *Voyager 1*, it was the second of the two spacecraft to arrive at Jupiter. *Voyager 1* reached Jupiter in March 1979, and *Voyager 2* reached the planet in July 1979.

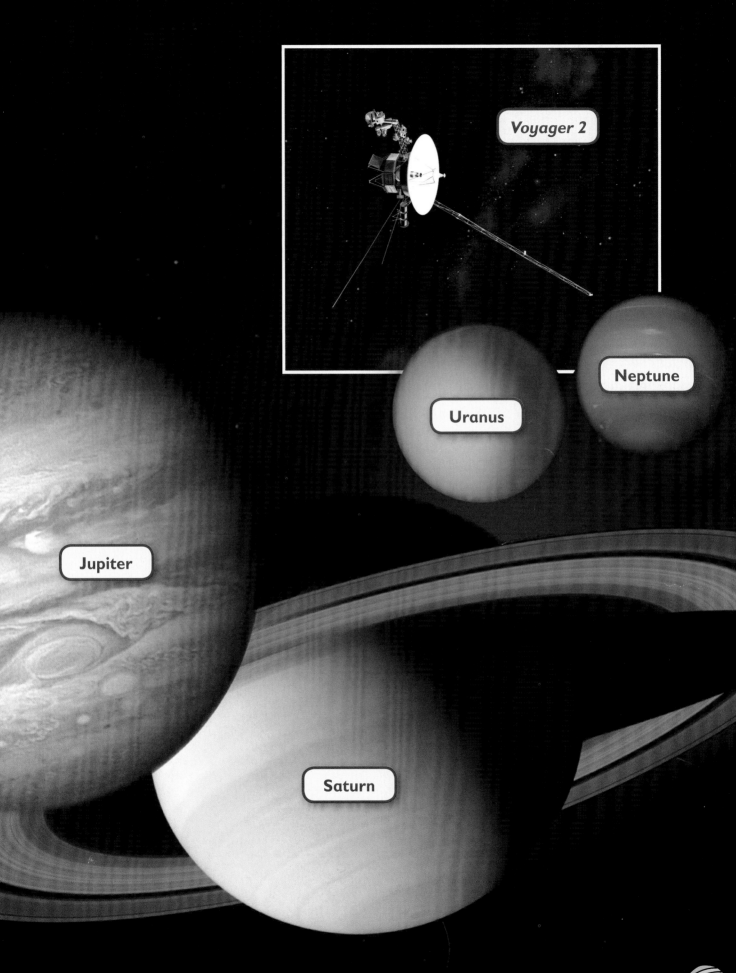

Voyager 2

Neptune

Uranus

Jupiter

Saturn

UNCOVERING NEPTUNE'S SECRETS

Voyager 2 **had traveled over 4.3 billion miles (7 billion km) when it reached distant Neptune on August 25, 1989.**

At its closest, *Voyager 2* flew just 3,075 miles (4,950 km) above Neptune's cloud tops. During its visit it discovered previously unknown moons and the planet's rings. The spacecraft measured wind speeds on Neptune and collected data that showed the chemical makeup of the planet. Finally, *Voyager 2* flew by Triton, revealing that the moon is home to cryovolcanoes and is one of the coldest places in the solar system.

After saying goodbye to Triton, *Voyager 2* was set on course for the outer reaches of the solar system, and beyond, deeper into our **galaxy**, the **Milky Way**. Its mission continues to this day!

While *Voyager 2*'s flyby of Neptune only lasted a matter of hours, without *Voyager 2*, very little would be known about Neptune, and books like this one would have far less information to give and few pictures of the faraway, blue world!

That's Out of This World!

Today, *Voyager 1* and *Voyager 2* are in the outer solar system heading in different directions. They are traveling a distance of about 300 million miles (500 million km) each year. Scientists expect that the two spacecraft will continue to send data back to Earth for another 20 or 30 years!

GLOSSARY

aligned (uh-LYND)
Placed or arranged in a straight line.

asteroids (AS-teh-roydz)
Rocky objects orbiting the Sun and ranging in size from a few feet (m) to hundreds of miles (km) in diameter.

astronomers (uh-STRAH-nuh-merz)
Scientists who specialize in the study of outer space.

atmosphere (AT-muh-sfeer)
The layer of gases surrounding a planet, moon, or star.

axis (AK-sus)
An imaginary line about which a body, such as a planet, rotates.

comet (KAH-mit)
An object orbiting the Sun consisting primarily of a center of ice and dust and, when the near the Sun, tails of gas and dust particles pointing away from the Sun.

craters (KRAY-turz)
Holes or dents in the surface of a planet or moon, usually caused by an impact with another space object, such as an asteroid.

cryovolcanoes (kry-oh-vol-KAY-nohz)
Volcanoes that release ice and cold liquids such as water, methane, and ammonia, instead of lava, which is hot, melted rock.

distortion (dih-STAWRT-shun)
A change in the shape of something.

equator (ih-KWAY-tur)
An imaginary line circling a body, such as a planet, which is an equal distance between its north and south poles.

galaxy (GA-lik-see)
A group of stars, dust, gas, and other objects held together in outer space by gravity.

gravity (GRA-vuh-tee)
The force that causes objects to be attracted toward Earth's center or toward other physical bodies in space, such as stars, planets, and moons.

Kuiper Belt (KY-per BELT)
A vast ring of icy, rocky objects that are orbiting the Sun beyond the orbit of Neptune.

Milky Way (MIL-kee WAY) The galaxy that includes Earth and the rest of our Sun's solar system.

moons (MOONZ)
Natural objects that orbit a planet.

myths (MITHS)
Stories told to explain something in nature or society, usually including supernatural beings or events.

nebulae (NEH-byuh-lee)
Massive clouds of gas and dust in outer space. Many nebulae are formed by the collapse of stars, releasing matter that may, over millions or billions of years, clump together to form new stars.

orbits (OR-bits) Circles around another object in a curved path.

planet (PLA-net) An object in space that is of a certain size and that orbits, or circles, a star.

solar system (SOH-ler SIS-tem)
The Sun and everything that orbits around it, including asteroids, meteoroids, comets, and the planets and their moons.

star (STAR) A body in space that produces its own heat and light through the release of nuclear energy created within its core.

WEBSITES

For web resources related to the subject of this book, go to: www.windmillbooks.com/weblinks and select this book's title.

READ MORE

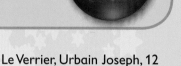

Roza, Greg. *Neptune: The Stormy Planet.* Our Solar System. New York: Gareth Stevens Leveled Readers, 2010.

Slade, Suzanne. *A Look at Neptune.* Astronomy Now! New York: PowerKids Press, 2007.

Winrich, Ralph. *Neptune.* The Solar System. Mankato, MN: Capstone Press, 2008.

INDEX